Mountain Peaks of Devotion

High above the world we stand,
A place where dreams touch land.
Whispers of the winds do call,
In our hearts, we hear it all.

Through the mist and rising sun,
We chase the heights, we are as one.
Every step is filled with grace,
In devotion, we find our place.

Climbing higher, we embrace,
The beauty found in nature's face.
A journey forged in trust and love,
Guided by the stars above.

Silken Nebulas of Aspiration

In the velvet night we gaze,
Finding hope in endless ways.
Silken threads of dreams unfold,
Stories of the brave and bold.

Each twinkling star, a wish to weave,
In the cosmos, we believe.
Aspiration lights our flight,
Taking shape in soft moonlight.

Beyond the clouds, our spirits soar,
Yearning for an open door.
In this dance of cosmic fire,
We ignite our heart's desire.

A Canvas of Burning Dreams

On a canvas rich and wide,
Colors clash and dreams collide.
Each stroke filled with fervent light,
Creating worlds both bold and bright.

Shades of passion paint the night,
Fueling our relentless fight.
With each layer, stories rise,
A reflection in the skies.

From shadows deep to brilliant hues,
Our spirit sings, forever true.
In this masterpiece we find,
The legacy of heart and mind.

Tidal Waves of Emotion

Crashing waves upon the shore,
Whispers of the heart's wild roar.
Tidal pulls of love and pain,
In this dance, we break the chain.

Every wave, a story told,
In their rhythm, the brave and bold.
Rising high, then pulling back,
Emotions flow on life's wide track.

Through the storms and calmest seas,
We learn the way our hearts appease.
In the depths, we seek the light,
Guided by the stars at night.

Arise from the Flames

From ashes we rise, unbowed and bold,
With hearts ignited, no longer cold.
The fire that burns, it fuels our dreams,
In shadows of doubt, we're bursting at seams.

The spark of hope lights our weary days,
Turning our fears into radiant rays.
With each step forward, we shed our past,
Emerging anew, our spirits vast.

Unfurling the Wings of Ambition

Like buds in spring, we yearn to soar,
Breaking the chains, reaching for more.
With dreams as our compass, we'll chart the skies,
Through storms and trials, our spirits rise.

Each challenge met is a lesson learned,
In the heart of the fire, our passion burned.
Unfurling wings, we chase the light,
With strength in our hearts, we take flight.

Momentous Leaps

With daring hearts, we jump and trust,
The ground below, a fleeting crust.
In every leap, we shed our fear,
For in the fall, our dreams draw near.

The edge we stand on, it's growth in disguise,
A leap of faith brings new sunrise.
Through valleys low, we find our way,
Each moment counts, come what may.

The Nature of Desire's Journey

Desire whispers softly, a call so sweet,
In the depths of our hearts, it finds its seat.
With each step forward, we tread unknown,
Chasing the dreams that feel like home.

Winding roads lead to paths unseen,
Through trials faced and battles keen.
In the nature of longing, we learn to thrive,
For desire's journey keeps dreams alive.

Flickering Shadows of Yearning

In quiet halls where whispers cling,
Shadows dance, hearts gently sing.
A glimpse of hope, a fleeting glance,
Yearning souls caught in a trance.

Beneath the stars, secrets unfold,
Dreams of warmth against the cold.
Lonely echoes in the night,
Flicker softly, dimly bright.

Pursuing the Light Within

Amidst the chaos and the noise,
A flicker glows, a silent voice.
Through tangled paths and winding ways,
Hope ignites, the spirit stays.

With every step, the shadows flee,
Illuminating what could be.
Chasing dreams through endless skies,
The light within, it never dies.

Ink and Ember

Words like fire, passion unfurled,
Casting spells within the world.
Ink and ember, a timeless dance,
In every stroke, a longing glance.

Pages whisper secrets told,
Crafted memories, dreams of gold.
With every scribble, hearts ignite,
Ink and ember, burning bright.

The Race with Affection's Ghost

In the twilight where shadows play,
Affection's ghost begins to sway.
A race through memories, sweet and pure,
Grasping moments, love's allure.

Footsteps echo on the ground,
In every heartbeat, love is found.
Chasing whispers, fleeting past,
A dance with ghosts, so swift, so fast.

The Pulse of Urgency

In shadows deep, we feel the chase,
Time ticks fast, a frantic pace.
Eyes wide open, hearts aflame,
Desire whispers, calls your name.

Moments fleeting, can't let go,
Every heartbeat, urgent flow.
Paths ignited, senses strained,
In this fervor, love is gained.

Ripples of Unfettered Love

A quiet stream begins to swell,
In currents deep, our secrets dwell.
With every wave, we build and break,
In every sigh, a promise we make.

Love's gentle touch, like silver light,
Shapes the shadows, soft and bright.
Unfettered hearts can roam so free,
In ripples deep, just you and me.

Through the Veil of Passion

Behind the curtain, flames ignite,
In whispered dreams, we take to flight.
With every glance, a world unfolds,
Our hearts entwined, a tale retold.

Beneath the stars, we dare to seek,
The language spoken, soft but bleak.
Through the veil, we find our way,
In passion's dance, we choose to stay.

Into the Heart's Wilderness

A forest thick, a hidden trail,
With every step, we tell our tale.
In wild embrace, we lose control,
The heart's wilderness, our eternal goal.

Among the thorns, blooms a rose,
Through tangled paths, true love grows.
In nature's arms, we'll find our truth,
In the wild, we rediscover youth.

Roads Weaving Through Sentiment

The winding paths of memory
Echo softly through the night.
Footsteps linger on each turn,
Whispers guide with gentle light.

Through shadowed corners of the mind,
Emotions dance with quiet grace.
Love and loss entwined in time,
Each road leads to a new place.

Faded photographs unfold,
Stories etched in every line.
In the heart, their warmth still glows,
A tapestry of love divine.

As sunrise paints the skies anew,
We walk together, hand in hand.
The roads we weave, a rich tableau,
In this journey, we shall stand.

The Fire Beneath the Surface

Smoldering coals in hidden depths,
A flicker stirs with passion's breath.
Unseen flames dance in silence,
Awaiting sparks to claim their heft.

With shadows cast by haunting dreams,
Desires burn like long-lost stars.
The heart ignites in quiet hours,
Each flicker tells of battle scars.

A blaze within that time can't tame,
It flickers, glows, and boldly fights.
In darkness, whispers call your name,
As embers blaze with restless light.

Thus, we feed the glow inside,
With memories that never fade.
The fire beneath will not subside,
In every heartbeat, love is made.

A Symphony of Abandon

In the stillness where we soar,
Chasing dreams in endless flight.
Notes of laughter fill the air,
As shadows melt into the night.

The rhythm of a heart laid bare,
Echoes soft like whispered vows.
With every leap, we cast aside,
The weight of what we've lost, but how?

Together in this wild embrace,
We dance beyond the world's demand.
In freedom's arms, we find our place,
A symphony both bright and grand.

So let us cast our fears away,
And ride the currents of our song.
In this abandon, we shall play,
Where all our hearts are bold and strong.

Veins of Color and Dream

Brushstrokes mingle on the canvas,
A world alive with vivid hues.
Boundless dreams take flight like birds,
In every shade, our hearts imbue.

A palette swirling through our souls,
Each color tells a story true.
With strokes of joy and swirls of sorrow,
Life's masterpiece begins anew.

Veins of passion pulse through time,
Connecting moments, strong and bright.
In every hue lies endless hope,
A tapestry of day and night.

So let us paint with every breath,
And dare to dream beyond the seam.
In color's embrace, we shall find,
A world alive, alive with dream.

The Way of the Unquenchable

In shadows deep, the fire glows,
A flicker bright, where longing flows.
The heart ignites with every sigh,
An echo soft, that will not die.

Through winds of change, the spirit soars,
Beyond the tide, through open doors.
With courage found in every trial,
We walk the path, enduring style.

Resonance in the Undergrowth

Among the leaves, a whisper sings,
A secret tune the wild heart brings.
Each rustle speaks of life below,
In tangled roots, the feelings grow.

The dance of shade, the light's embrace,
In hidden nooks, a sacred space.
The earth respire, the saplings thrive,
In harmony, all souls derive.

Cascades of Intense Emotion

Flowing waters, swirling deep,
A torrent strong, where sorrows weep.
Each wave a tale of love and loss,
In rippling depths, we bear the cross.

The pounding heart, an endless stream,
In moments caught, we chase the dream.
Through cliffs and canyons, feelings soar,
A symphony of evermore.

Sinfonia of Heart and Earth

In twilight's glow, the world takes flight,
Unveiling truths beneath the night.
Each heartbeat calls, a melody sweet,
With nature's pulse, our lives repeat.

The mountains rise, the valleys sing,
In every breath, we find the spring.
The earth and heart, forever twined,
In this sinfonia, love we find.

Starlit Aspirations

Under the vast and twinkling sky,
Dreams take flight, learning to fly.
Each star a wish, a silent plea,
Chasing visions of what could be.

In the quiet of the night, we stand,
With longing hearts and open hands.
The universe whispers sweet and low,
Igniting flames in the hearts aglow.

As we wander paths unknown,
Through trials faced, seeds are sown.
Illuminate the dark with hope,
Together, we learn, together, we cope.

In starlit dreams, we'll find our way,
Guided by light, come what may.
With every step into the night,
Our aspirations take their flight.

Beyond the Horizon of Hope

Waves crash softly against the shore,
Each whisper speaks of dreams in store.
The horizon beckons, calling clear,
To venture forth, to conquer fear.

Beyond that line where sky meets sea,
Lay the treasures, waiting for me.
With each sunrise, a chance anew,
In the warmth of light, I start to pursue.

Clouds may gather, storms may roar,
Yet hope's soft voice will restore.
For beyond the tempest's loud decree,
Lies the calm and the mystery.

So I'll sail forth, brave and bold,
Finding richness in stories untold.
Each wave a promise, each breeze a sigh,
Beyond the horizon, I'll learn to fly.

The Call of the Soul

In moments still, the whispers rise,
Echoes of truths beneath the skies.
The soul's soft call, a gentle guide,
Leading us to where dreams abide.

With every heartbeat, a story woven,
Lost in the light of the sun, golden.
Dance through shadows, embrace the light,
For within the darkness, stars shine bright.

Listen closely, let the silence speak,
In the depths of the heart, we seek.
With every step, our wisdom grows,
Unraveling paths no one else knows.

So heed the call, the inner voice,
In the journey of life, I rejoice.
For within me lies the sacred whole,
Forever guided by the call of the soul.

Currents of Devotion

In every gesture, love flows free,
Currents of warmth, a gentle sea.
With every heartbeat, a bond so true,
In whispers soft, I cherish you.

Through storms and calm, together we stand,
Life's raw beauty held in our hands.
Devotion shines like a guiding star,
In the darkest hours, never too far.

Moments shared, both big and small,
Each one a treasure, a radiant call.
Through life's ebb and its relentless flow,
In the depths of love, we continue to grow.

So here's to the journey, the tides that blend,
Currents of devotion that never end.
With open hearts, we build our dream,
Together we rise, a steadfast team.

Trail of Euphoria

In the meadow, flowers bloom,
Dancing gently, chasing the moon.
Whispers sweet upon the air,
Joyful hearts lay themselves bare.

Winding paths of golden light,
Lift our spirits, take our flight.
In each moment, laughter sings,
Hopeful dreams on vibrant wings.

With every step, the world unfolds,
Stories waiting to be told.
Embrace the warmth, the vibrant hue,
In the trail of euphoria, we'll continue.

Through the valleys, over time,
We find rhythm, pulse, and rhyme.
Hand in hand, forever roam,
In this bliss, we've found our home.

Chasing the Flame

In the night, a flicker glows,
A warm embrace as spirit flows.
With every spark, the shadows fight,
Chasing dreams towards the light.

Fingers stretch through the dark,
Yearning for that vibrant spark.
In the glow, our fears release,
Chaos fades, we find our peace.

Hearts ignited, wild and free,
Pursuing all we wish to be.
Through the storms, we cast away,
Guided by the flame's ballet.

In this dance, we shall find,
The treasures that our souls enshrined.
Chasing the flame, we unite,
Together, we will rise in flight.

Footsteps of Longing

Upon the shore, soft waves break,
Each echo a tender ache.
Tracing paths in shifting sand,
Whispers of what hearts withstand.

In the distance, shadows call,
Figures standing, rise and fall.
Memories cling, like autumn leaves,
Lost in time, the heart believes.

With every step, a silent plea,
Seeking solace, yearning to be free.
In each breath, a story we share,
Footsteps of longing lead us there.

As twilight paints the evening sky,
We wander on, and there we sigh.
In this journey, hearts shall sing,
Of all the love that longing brings.

Awakening the Muse

In the quiet of dawn's embrace,
Ideas swirl like a gentle grace.
Brush in hand, a canvas bare,
Awakening the muse, beyond compare.

Colors dance in vibrant hue,
Each stroke brings the vision through.
In the stillness, inspiration calls,
Whispers echo within the walls.

Let the spirit soar and fly,
Creating worlds that never die.
With every word, a heartbeat thrums,
Awakening wonders, and bliss it hums.

Through the art, our souls ignite,
In the shadows, we find our light.
Awakening the muse, we see,
The beauty in our tapestry.

Dancing on the Edge of Tomorrow

Footsteps echo, soft and light,
A rhythm born of dreams in flight.
Chasing whispers, futures bright,
We twirl beneath the stars' delight.

Hearts entwined in the midnight air,
Each moment, fragile, beyond compare.
With every leap, we shed our care,
Embracing all that life might dare.

The Canvas of Hope and Fire

Brush strokes vivid, colors swirl,
Painting visions, futures unfurl.
In shadows deep, bright embers gleam,
Crafting a world from the heart's dream.

Flames of courage ignite the night,
In every stroke, the will to fight.
A tapestry woven with endless might,
Hope ignites, setting souls alight.

A Beacon Through the Night

In the stillness, a light so pure,
Guiding lost souls, steady and sure.
Through veils of darkness, hope takes flight,
A flame that flickers, burning bright.

Voices whisper, echoing near,
In the silence, we conquer fear.
Together we stand, hearts sincere,
As long as the beacon's light is here.

Resonating Through the Uncharted

Waves of mystery crash and flow,
In silence profound, intuitions grow.
Paths untraveled, we venture wide,
Hearts ignited, with love as our guide.

Echoes linger in the dance of fate,
As stardust weaves a world innate.
Through the unknown, we navigate,
With dreams that soar and never wait.

Journey of Fire

In the heart of the blaze, we dance and we roam,
With sparks in our eyes, it feels like a home.
Through shadows and light, we forge our own fate,
Each flicker and flare seals our bond, it's innate.

The flames whisper secrets, old tales from the past,
With courage ignited, we know we'll last.
Every ember a promise, a dream to ignite,
On this journey of fire, we'll chase the bright light.

Heart's Compass

In the silence of whispers, true love's direction,
A compass of feelings, guiding connection.
With every heartbeat, we follow its call,
Through valleys and peaks, together we'll crawl.

In shadows of doubt, our spirits unite,
A journey of trust, through day and through night.
The way may get tangled, but never we part,
Our heart is the compass, our map is the heart.

The Way of Desire

In the depths of longing, a fire does gleam,
With every soft glance, we fulfill the dream.
The pull of connection, an unspoken word,
On this path of desire, our spirits are stirred.

We chase the horizon, with passion as guide,
In moments of silence, our feelings reside.
With every step closer, our souls intertwine,
In the way of desire, your heart is like mine.

Embers in the Night

Beneath the vast sky, where shadows take flight,
We gather the embers that glow through the night.
With whispers of starlight, we share our dreams,
In the quiet of darkness, everything gleams.

As the hours drift by, in soft quiet grace,
We find warmth in the fire, in this sacred space.
Together we linger, with hopes shining bright,
In the dance of the embers, we own the night.

Unfolding Mysteries of Desire

In shadows deep, where secrets play,
Whispers dance in soft decay.
Hearts entwined, a fragile thread,
Yearning blooms, where silence tread.

Fingers brush on velvet dream,
Emotions pulse, a silent scream.
Beneath the moon's soft, watchful gaze,
Desire's light in twilight's haze.

A gaze that lingers, tender, fierce,
Promises soft, the heart they pierce.
Each moment held, a stolen sigh,
In the depths where shadows lie.

Lost in echoes, time stands still,
Awakening a longing thrill.
Every heartbeat, a step explored,
In these mysteries, we're adored.

The Allure of Tangled Trails

Through winding paths, we lose our way,
In tangled woods where shadows play.
Nature's voice a beckon clear,
With every turn, we draw near.

Leaves whisper secrets, tales untold,
In the embrace of green and gold.
Footsteps soft on earthy ground,
In every rustle, magic found.

Sunlight dances on the streams,
Crafting visions from our dreams.
Each twist and turn, a chance to feel,
The heart's desire, the soul's appeal.

Adventure calls in sweet refrain,
In tangled trails, we break the chain.
Together we wander, hand in hand,
In nature's grasp, forever stand.

Journeying Through a Heartbeat

Each heartbeat drifts on waves of time,
Rhythms echo, soft and sublime.
With every pulse, a story grows,
In silent spaces, love bestows.

Footfalls whisper on the way,
Every moment, a bright bouquet.
In colorful hues, dreams ignite,
Painting skies with purest light.

A glance exchanged, a spark, a trust,
In this journey, it's a must.
With gentle hands, we weave our fate,
In each heartbeat, we create.

Through valleys deep and mountains tall,
Together we rise, together we fall.
In the rhythm of each shared sigh,
Love's sweet journey lifts us high.

The Thrill of the Uncharted

Beyond horizons, dreams await,
In uncharted lands, we elevate.
With joyful hearts, we venture forth,
Exploring depths of untamed worth.

Stars above, like candles glow,
Guiding paths where wanderers go.
Every step, a tale unspooled,
In adventures wild, we are schooled.

The air is thick with promise bright,
With every breath, we chase the light.
Fear dissolves in the lover's call,
For in the unknown, we stand tall.

New vistas call, we heed their voice,
In every challenge, we rejoice.
Boundless spirits, we set our sail,
In the thrill of the uncharted trail.

Flares of Inspiration

In shadows deep where visions spark,
A flicker bright ignites the dark.
With courage found in silent cries,
The heart takes flight, the spirit flies.

Through pages worn and ink so bold,
Stories waiting to be told.
From whispered winds to thunder's roar,
Inspiration breathes, forevermore.

A canvas stretched, a brush in hand,
Colors dance where dreams expand.
In every note, in every line,
Flares of light, the soul divine.

So let us chase the blazing trails,
Where hope prevails and love entails.
With open hearts, we'll share the flame,
Flares of inspiration, never tame.

Whispers of Yearning

In the quiet of the night,
Where stars shimmer, soft and bright.
A voice calls out, a gentle plea,
Whispers of yearning, wild and free.

Echoes of dreams that drift away,
In every sigh, a heart's ballet.
With shadows long and moments few,
Yearning whispers, sweet and true.

A fleeting touch, a lover's gaze,
In this dance, we long to stay.
Through time's embrace, we weave our fate,
Whispers linger, never late.

A secret bond, a thread so fine,
In every heartbeat, yours and mine.
Through storms we run, through skies we sail,
Whispers of yearning tell our tale.

The Thrum of Existence

In the pulse of life, a steady beat,
Each moment felt, each breath, a treat.
Through laughter bright and sorrow's fall,
The thrum of existence calls us all.

From mountains high to oceans deep,
In every tear, in every leap.
The joys and pains, the ebb and flow,
Existence thrums, and we all grow.

In every soul, a fire's glow,
Through dawn's embrace and twilight's show.
Life's vibrant dance, both fierce and kind,
The thrum of existence, intertwined.

So let us cherish every sound,
In silence lost, in chaos found.
With open hearts, we heed the song,
The thrum of existence, where we belong.

Terrain of Dreamers

Across the hills where visions soar,
In fields of hope, we yearn for more.
The terrain of dreamers stretches wide,
Where passions bloom and fears abide.

With every step, the ground we shape,
A journey bold, a daring escape.
From whispers soft to shouts of glee,
In this realm, we are set free.

Through winding paths and secret glades,
We seek the light as doubt soon fades.
In twilight's glow, our spirits rise,
The terrain of dreamers, where magic lies.

So let us wander, hand in hand,
Together we'll explore this land.
With hearts aglow and visions clear,
The terrain of dreamers, forever near.

Cascade of Intensified Moments

In the river's gentle flow,
Time dances with the breeze,
Every glance a fleeting glow,
Whispers carried through the trees.

Moments build like waterfall,
Rushing forth from peaks so high,
Echoes in the silence call,
As shadows lengthen, dreams fly.

Each drop sparkles in the light,
Memories like diamonds shine,
Caught in nature's pure delight,
Forever etched, yours and mine.

Through the mist, our steps align,
Holding tight as currents shift,
In this dance, our souls entwine,
Moments shared are love's great gift.

Flames on the Horizon

At dusk, the sky begins to change,
Colors spill like molten gold,
Whispers of a world so strange,
In every heart, a story told.

Flames flicker on the edge of night,
Brighter than the stars' embrace,
Burning with a fierce delight,
Illuminating every space.

Hope ignites in hearts once cold,
Passions rise like tides that sway,
In the warmth, we feel the bold,
Embers guide us on our way.

As darkness yields to morning's grace,
The flames will shape our path anew,
Together, we will find our place,
In the glow of dreams so true.

The Journey of the Heart

Upon the road, two souls embark,
With every step, their bond will grow,
Through light and shadow, love's own spark,
Together facing all they sow.

With laughter shared, and tears that blend,
They navigate the twists and turns,
Each moment rich, they comprehend,
With every lesson, passion burns.

Mountains high and valleys low,
In tandem they will brave the climb,
Their love, a river's steady flow,
Surpassing even space and time.

Through storms and sun, they journey on,
Embracing every bittersweet,
For in their hearts, the light has shone,
A testament to love's heartbeat.

Sparks in the Twilight

As daylight fades and shadows grow,
The sky ignites in shades of pink,
In whispered winds, a secret flow,
Where thoughts take flight and hearts can think.

In twilight's glow, the world feels near,
With every color, dreams unwind,
A dance of joy, a tinge of fear,
In the magic of the dusk, we bind.

Tiny sparks like stars ignite,
In the canvas of the evening air,
Moments stitched in love's soft light,
A tapestry beyond compare.

As darkness falls, we find our way,
With sparks alight in every heart,
In twilight's grace, we choose to stay,
A journey formed, never to part.

Threads of Intensity

In the quiet night, we weave our dreams,
Threads of silver glow like moonlit streams.
Whispers in shadows, secrets untold,
Binding our hearts with a power bold.

Each heartbeat echoes, a rhythm profound,
Intertwined fates in the silence abound.
Visions aflame, in the dark they ignite,
Threads of intensity, fueling the night.

The tapestry grows, with colors so bright,
Pain and pleasure dance in the soft twilight.
Hope interlaces with memories dear,
Binding our souls, we conquer our fear.

Together we stand, as the world fades away,
In the heart of the storm, we find our way.
A fabric of passion and endless delight,
Threads of intensity, our guiding light.

Radiant Pursuit

Chasing the dawn, the sun in our eyes,
Every step forward, a gift in disguise.
Through valleys of shadows, we run hand in hand,
In this radiant pursuit, together we stand.

Moments of laughter, like stars in the void,
Filling our spirits, each doubt is destroyed.
Journeying onward, with every sweet breath,
With love as our compass, defying all death.

The horizon beckons, painting skies anew,
Colors of passion, vibrant and true.
Boundless ambition, like winds that resound,
In this radiant pursuit, our hearts are unbound.

So let us keep running, no path is too steep,
For dreams ignite fires that ignite in our sleep.
Together we'll flourish, our spirits in flight,
In the radiant glow of the welcoming light.

Steps to the Infinite

Each step we take on this winding road,
Leads us to places where dreams are bestowed.
In whispers of fate, the universe sings,
Steps to the infinite, oh the joy it brings.

With eyes on the stars, we wander and roam,
Finding the magic that calls us back home.
Through trials and triumphs, we learn and we grow,
A dance with the cosmos, forever in flow.

Time bends around us, a wonderful quilt,
Woven with moments, no thread ever built.
Embracing the now, as we reach for the skies,
Steps to the infinite, where destiny lies.

So take my hand gently, let's walk through the night,
With hearts intertwined, we'll soar to new heights.
Unravel the mystery, this life's grand design,
In steps to the infinite, our souls brightly shine.

Dance of the Heart

In the moon's soft glow, let our passions ignite,
A delicate dance in the velvety night.
Every heartbeat echoes, a rhythm so sweet,
In the dance of the heart, two souls gently meet.

With each turn and sway, the world fades away,
Lost in the music, we find our own way.
Eyes locked in promise, a silent refrain,
In the dance of the heart, love conquers all pain.

Around us the stars twinkle brightly above,
Bearing witness to this enchanting love.
In a world full of chaos, we create our own art,
Embracing the magic, it's the dance of the heart.

So hold me close now, let our spirit take flight,
As we twirl through the shadows, our futures ignite.
In the rhythm of life, we'll never depart,
Together forever, in the dance of the heart.

Embracing the Unraveled Road

With footsteps light on twisted trails,
We wander free where silence sails.
The bends ahead, unknown and wide,
In faith, we walk, our hearts our guide.

In shadows deep where whispers dwell,
The stories rise, like tales to tell.
We greet the dawn with open eyes,
And dance beneath the endless skies.

Through valleys low and mountains high,
With every breath, we'll learn to fly.
Embracing all that life can bring,
We find our song and start to sing.

So here we stand, no fear, no shame,
Each path we choose ignites a flame.
With every step, we break the mold,
On this unraveled road, we're bold.

Luminous Steps Across Time

In whispered hues, the past awakes,
With each soft glow, the silence breaks.
Steps etched in light, where shadows creep,
We find the truths that time will keep.

Through ages lost, our hearts entwined,
With every moment, fate aligned.
A dance of stars, a tale retold,
Across the night, our souls unfold.

With dreams aglow, we pave the way,
For tomorrow's dawn, a bright array.
In luminous trails, we'll redefine,
Our footprints linger, pure and divine.

Together we forge a radiant path,
As time dissolves the aftermath.
In every glance, a spark ignites,
And shines eternal through our nights.

Echoes of an Undying Flame

Within the heart, a fire burns bright,
Its embers dance in the soft moonlight.
Through storms and trials, it stands so bold,
An undying flame, a tale to be told.

In whispered songs, it calls our name,
A beacon fierce, it stirs the same.
With every flicker, memories swell,
In echoes deep, forever dwell.

We gather close, our spirits soar,
As warmth surrounds, we crave for more.
With hands held tight, we fuel the light,
A bond unbroken, through day and night.

And when the world turns cold and dim,
We'll find our strength, no need to swim.
For in our hearts, that flame shall rise,
An endless glow beneath the skies.

Starlit Pursuit

Beneath the cloak of midnight's grace,
We chase the stars, a boundless space.
With every step, the cosmos calls,
In a dance of dreams, our spirit falls.

Through whispered winds, our wishes soar,
In starlit paths, we seek for more.
With open hearts and glimmering eyes,
We chase the light where magic lies.

In every twinkle, hope aligns,
A tapestry of fate entwines.
Together we weave this cosmic thread,
With starlit hearts, no fear or dread.

So let us run, through night and day,
In pursuit of dreams, come what may.
For with the stars, our souls ignite,
In starlit pursuit, we find the light.

Threads of Fiery Intent

In the loom of dreams we weave,
Threads of passion interleave.
With every heartbeat, colors flare,
Intentions bright, a dance laid bare.

Through the fire, our spirits burn,
In the heat, we make our turn.
Woven tales of love and strife,
Threads of intent, the fabric of life.

In shadows cast, we find our light,
Twists and turns in the velvet night.
Embers fly as hopes take flight,
A tapestry of radiant might.

Each thread a story, bold and new,
Intertwined, hearts' rhythm true.
Fate's gentle hand, it leads the way,
Threads of fiery intent, come what may.

Whispers of the Soul's Journey

In silence deep, the whispers call,
Echoes tender, we rise and fall.
The soul's journey, a winding road,
In every step, a heavy load.

Beneath the stars, the heart takes flight,
Guided by dreams in the still of night.
Each whisper holds a piece of light,
Illuminating shadows, shining bright.

Through valleys low and mountains high,
We seek the truth, we learn to fly.
With every breath, the spirit grows,
In whispers soft, our journey flows.

The path unfolds, we walk alone,
Yet hearts entwined, we find our home.
In every moment, grace appears,
Whispers of the soul, calming fears.

Dance of Endless Longing

In the twilight, shadows play,
A dance of longing, come what may.
Hearts entwined in the softest sway,
Yearning souls in hues of gray.

With every step, a dream takes hold,
A story whispered, a memory told.
Moonlit glances, promises bold,
In this dance, our hearts unfold.

The rhythm pulses, a timeless beat,
In the silence, we find our heat.
Each twirl a promise, we won't retreat,
Endless longing, bittersweet.

Together we spin, lost in time,
In the dance, our hearts do rhyme.
With every breath, the night is long,
A dance of longing, a haunting song.

The Chase of Radiant Hues

Upon the hill where sunsets glow,
We chase the colors, fierce and slow.
Radiant hues paint the wide expanse,
In every stroke, a daring dance.

Through fields of gold, we freely roam,
In the splendor, we find our home.
Touches of crimson, whispers of blue,
In the chase, our spirits renew.

A canvas wide, the world a stage,
Where dreams ignite and hearts engage.
With every ray, the dawn breaks through,
In the chase of radiant hues.

The sky ablaze, we lift our eyes,
To chase the beauty that never dies.
In artful brush, the moments fuse,
Together we paint, in radiant hues.

The Echo of Hearts Awakened

In the hush of twilight's grace,
Whispers rise, a soft embrace.
Echoed thoughts, a sweet refrain,
Hearts awaken, free from pain.

Stars ignite the velvet sky,
Hopeful hearts begin to fly.
In the silence, love's decree,
Binding souls, you and me.

Time suspends, each moment gleams,
Life unfolds in vibrant dreams.
Hand in hand, we dare to seek,
The echo speaks, the heart is meek.

Through the shadows, light will guide,
Inward journeys, side by side.
Every sigh, a promise made,
In the echo, love won't fade.

Paths Woven with Dreams

In the forest, trails unfurl,
Magic whispers, flags unfurl.
Steps of faith on paths unknown,
Woven dreams, seeds carefully sown.

Beneath the stars, our thoughts align,
Find the patterns, seek the sign.
Dancing leaves and gentle streams,
Every step, a dance of dreams.

With each heartbeat, courage flows,
Facing fears, the spirit grows.
In the tapestry of night,
Hope illuminates our flight.

Together we will forge the way,
Through the storms, come what may.
Onward, upward, hearts ablaze,
Paths entwined in endless praise.

The Enlightened Pursuit

In the quest for truth we roam,
Finding solace in the unknown.
Every question, a chance to learn,
In the struggle, wisdom's turn.

With each sunrise, insights bloom,
Chasing shadows, dispelling gloom.
The heart, a compass, leads us right,
Guiding souls through day and night.

Fingers touch the fabric real,
Moments shared, the world we feel.
In this dance, a sacred trust,
Through the chaos, love is just.

Together we will seek the light,
In the darkness, hearts ignite.
Enlightened in this pursuit,
Life unfolds, absolute truth.

Carving a Path of Dreams

In twilight's breath, paths softly glow,
Footsteps whisper where hopes shall flow.
Stars align in the silent night,
Chasing shadows, we seek the light.

Winds of change gently guide our way,
Through tangled woods, we long to stay.
Each turn reveals a tale anew,
In every heartbeat, a dream breaks through.

With courage sewn in the fabric of fate,
We carve our dreams while it's not too late.
Through valleys deep, over mountains steep,
We gather strength from the dreams we keep.

And when the dawn breaks the veil of sleep,
In the rich soil, our hopes we'll reap.
Together we stand, with hearts ablaze,
Carving a path through life's winding maze.

The Thrum of the Unseen

In quiet corners, a pulse alive,
Whispers of stories, in shadows, they thrive.
An echo of dreams, reverberates clear,
A tapestry woven with threads of fear.

Beneath the surface, the currents sway,
Invisible hands guide our way.
In the stillness, a symphony plays,
The thrum of the unseen, in myriad ways.

Each heartbeat resonates, a gentle hum,
A call from the depths, to what's yet to come.
In silence, we listen, the messages flow,
The unseen may guide, if only we know.

As day turns to night, and shadows grow long,
We find our strength in this hidden song.
For in the unseen, there's magic to find,
A thrum of connection, heart to heart, intertwined.

A Frenzy of Bright Moments

In the rush of laughter, the spark ignites,
Moments flash by like celestial lights.
Dancing in daylight, joy finds its place,
A frenzy of brightness, that time can't erase.

With each fleeting second, a memory blooms,
Colors exploding, in vibrant costumes.
We chase after glimmers, in sunbeam's embrace,
In a whirlwind of wonders, we quicken our pace.

The heart skips a beat, as the world spins around,
In the chaos of joy, pure solace is found.
In every heartbeat, we weave a new thread,
A tapestry bright, in which we are led.

And when the dusk settles, and day bids goodbye,
We carry those moments, like stars in the sky.
For in the frenzy, the laughter, the tears,
We find our true selves, transcending our fears.

Shadows Cast by Intensity

In the glow of the flame, shadows dance wide,
Embers flicker as passions collide.
With fervent whispers, the night draws near,
Shadows cast tightly, hiding our fear.

The weight of the silence can spark the loud,
In the depth of the night, every heartbeat proud.
Through the veil of the dark, intensity grows,
A fierce illumination that only one knows.

As colors bleed into the fabric of night,
Shadows stretch long in the fading light.
In the richness of moments that fervently stay,
The shadows remind us, in their own way.

For every intensity, a shadow remains,
A dance of light woven through joys and pains.
And in the embrace of both dark and bright,
We find our true essence, our soul's sacred light.

Between the Heartbeats

In silence, the whispers linger low,
Fleeting moments, shadows in tow.
Time dances softly, a fleeting guest,
Caught between rhythms, our hearts at rest.

A glance exchanged, a secret shared,
Between the beats, a truth declared.
In the pause, our souls align,
To find the meaning, so divine.

Echoes of laughter fill the air,
In the quiet, we find our prayer.
Every heartbeat pulses in tune,
Beneath the watchful gaze of the moon.

With every sigh, we drift and dream,
In the spaces, a gentle gleam.
Held in the stillness, we are free,
Between the heartbeats, you and me.

An Odyssey of the Yearning

In the depths of night, we search the skies,
With hopes like stars, we rise and fly.
Yearning for love, a distant shore,
Each wave whispers tales of yore.

Through valleys deep, where shadows creep,
In the echoes, our secrets keep.
A journey mapped by longing's hand,
To find our place, to understand.

With every heartbeat, a call to roam,
In the wilderness, we make our home.
Embers flicker, dreams take flight,
An odyssey born from the depths of night.

As dawn approaches, we chase the light,
Leaving behind the remnants of night.
For in the yearning, we find our way,
Guided by love, come what may.

The Light of Infinite Explorations

In the vast expanse, horizons gleam,
Each step a promise, each dawn a dream.
Through valleys carved by time's gentle hand,
We chase the light across the land.

With whispered winds, our spirits soar,
Every heartbeat yearning for more.
In the silence, the answers bloom,
In the shadows, dispelling gloom.

Voices of wonder call us near,
In the wanderlust, we shed our fear.
For every journey ignites the flame,
Of infinite paths, none are the same.

Step by step, we claim our quest,
In the dance of life, we seek the best.
With the light as our guide, we roam free,
In endless explorations, you and me.

Prism of Emotion

Through the prism, colors blend and sway,
Emotion's dance on a bright display.
Each hue a feeling, deep and true,
In the spectrum of life, I find you.

Joy sparkles bright like the sun at noon,
While gentler shades hum a tender tune.
In every flicker, laughter and tears,
In the chaos, the beauty appears.

Love wraps around like a warm embrace,
Colors entwining in life's great race.
Every heartbeat paints the skies,
With shades of longing, where passion lies.

Through shadows cast by doubts and fears,
The prism shines, dissolving tears.
Together we'll weave a tapestry bold,
In the art of emotion, our story told.

The Art of Pursuit

In the shadow of the moonlight glow,
Silent whispers guide us slow.
Every step a dance, a chance we take,
The heart's compass, never to break.

Fingers tracing paths unknown,
In the night's embrace, we have grown.
Chasing echoes of a distant song,
Together, we are where we belong.

Moments captured in fleeting time,
The rhythm of love, a gentle rhyme.
Each glance a promise, a spark ignites,
In the art of pursuit, our love unites.

Through valleys deep and hills so high,
We'll chase the horizon, touch the sky.
In every heartbeat, there's a quest,
Forever pursuing, never at rest.

Heartbeats in Motion

Two souls entwined, a vivid beat,
Each pulse a story, life so sweet.
In quiet moments, words unspoken,
Heartbeats in motion, never broken.

A dance of trust beneath the stars,
Navigating dreams, healing scars.
Every glance, a vivid sign,
Our love's momentum, forever entwined.

Through storms we wander, hand in hand,
With every challenge, we understand.
Together we are strong and bold,
Heartbeats in motion, a tale retold.

In the silence that speaks so loud,
We find our strength among the crowd.
With every moment, time stands still,
In heartbeats, we chase love's thrill.

The Trail of Desire

Faint whispers drift upon the breeze,
Leading us through the whispering trees.
Each step we take is a path anew,
On the trail of desire, me and you.

Sunset hues paint the twilight sky,
With every breath, we aim to fly.
Through tangled woods and fields so wide,
With love as our guide, we decide.

The light of passion ignites our way,
In the stillness, we choose to stay.
Every heartbeat quickens the chase,
On the trail of desire, we find our place.

Moments linger like fragrant blooms,
Filling our hearts with sweet perfumes.
In the echoes of tomorrow's glow,
On this trail, together we'll grow.

Chasing Ember Dreams

In the twilight of our whispered hopes,
We dance upon the edges, the slopes.
Chasing ember dreams, a flickering light,
Guiding our souls through the night.

Like fireflies in the summer's sheen,
We follow trails where we have been.
Every moment, a spark, a flame,
In the chase, love's essence remains.

With open hearts, we leap and sway,
Ember dreams lighting the way.
Through valleys deep and skies so vast,
In chasing dreams, we find our past.

Together we soar on whispered wings,
In the silence, the freedom sings.
Chasing ember dreams, hand in hand,
In our hearts forever, you understand.

Etched in the Fire's Glow

Crimson embers spark and fly,
Whispers of the past float high,
In the hearth where stories dwell,
Ancient tales in flames they tell.

Shadows dance upon the wall,
Echoes linger, rise and fall,
Moments captured in the light,
Etched in fire, shining bright.

Flickering warmth on weathered skin,
Memories weave where dreams begin,
A flick of hope, a breath of air,
In the glow, our secrets share.

Through the ash, a vision clear,
Fiery paths draw us near,
Together in this fierce embrace,
Etched in time, a sacred space.

Dance of the Unforged

In the silence, metal waits,
Shaped by hands that forge our fates,
Cold and still, yet full of fire,
Dreams of strength, a hidden desire.

Anvil's song through night and day,
Shimmering sparks that find their way,
Dance of steel, a wild embrace,
Transforming time, revealing grace.

Crafting beauty from the grind,
Nature's rhythms, intertwined,
Each strike a pulse, each turn a dance,
Unforged love seeks its chance.

Whispers echo, metal moans,
Fires burn, carving bones,
In the heat, we find our form,
Dance of life, both fierce and warm.

Unstoppable Crescendo

A whisper grows into a roar,
Tides of sound crash on the shore,
In the heart, a rhythm beats,
Unstoppable, the passion meets.

Echoes surge through open skies,
Notes entwine where freedom flies,
Every voice a thread unique,
Together strong, we rise and speak.

Symphony of hope and dread,
In the swell, our spirits fed,
Chasing dreams like wild winds blow,
Unstoppable, our spirits glow.

Resonating through the night,
Harmony, our boundless flight,
Feel the pulse, the vibrant glow,
Unstoppable, let the music flow.

The Unraveled Thread of Life

A tapestry frayed at the seams,
Woven with whispers, hopes, and dreams,
In the light, stories unwind,
The thread of life, complex, entwined.

Colors fade and shadows creep,
Memories linger, secrets keep,
Each knot a moment, tightly wound,
Unraveled paths through time abound.

Stitches break, yet still we mend,
Through the struggles, we ascend,
Patterns change, our journey's plight,
In every tear, we find our light.

A thread unspooled beneath the stars,
Life's threads weaving near and far,
In the chaos, beauty thrives,
The unraveled thread of vibrant lives.

In Search of the Heart's Compass

In silent whispers, dreams unfold,
Through tangled paths of stories told.
The compass guides with gentle grace,
In search of love, we find our place.

With every step, the shadows dance,
A flicker of hope, a fleeting chance.
We wander far, yet yearn to stay,
As stars above begin to sway.

Through valleys deep, and mountains high,
The heart will search, it will not lie.
Mapping love's terrain, each beat a guide,
In the quest for truth, we'll not divide.

In search of warmth, where hearts align,
A journey etched in love's own sign.
Amidst the storms, we learn to steer,
To find the path that draws us near.

Unwavering Current of Desire

Rising tides, a heart aflame,
Whispers soft, yet bold the name.
In every glance, sparks fly anew,
An unwavering path, both bright and true.

Through restless nights, the fantasies spark,
Bathed in moonlight, igniting the dark.
With passion's touch, we claim the night,
Driven by dreams, we take our flight.

In the dance of souls, a rhythm found,
Our spirits soar, unbound and unbound.
Chasing echoes, we navigate,
The currents strong, yet we await.

Through love's tempest, we are the sail,
Guided by yearning, we will prevail.
With every beat, our hearts inspire,
Boundless loves, igniting fire.

Stepping Stones in the Twilight

Under twilight's soft embrace,
We tread on stones, a sacred space.
Each step a whisper, a tale unfolds,
In shadows thick, our courage molds.

With twilight's hues, the world transforms,
Embracing change, as silence warms.
Each stone a memory, a bridge we weave,
Guiding us forth, as dreams believe.

In gentle murmurs, the night calls near,
Navigating paths, we cast aside fear.
With every heartbeat, we find our way,
In the light of dusk, we choose to stay.

For in the dusk, our spirits soar,
With stepping stones, we long for more.
As daylight fades, we boldly roam,
In twilight's arms, we find our home.

Chasing the Horizon's Flame

Beyond the hills, the sunset glows,
With every stride, our fervor grows.
Chasing colors as day gives way,
To horizon's flame, where dreams will play.

In the twilight's kiss, we run so free,
With fire in hearts, wild as the sea.
Each step we take, on paths unknown,
In pursuit of grace, we are reborn.

Embers flicker, guiding our quest,
As shadows merge, we find our rest.
In chasing light, we again ignite,
The burning hope, our spirits bright.

Through twilight's layers, we paint the night,
With radiant dreams, our souls take flight.
Forever seeking, with passion's name,
We hold the joy of chasing flame.

Waves of Zeal

Feel the tide washing in,
Casting dreams on the shore.
With each surge, a fresh spin,
Awakening hearts to explore.

Rolling whispers of light,
Chasing shadows, making space.
In the moon's gentle sight,
Passion dances with grace.

An echo of laughter bright,
In the depths of the sea.
With the dawn's early light,
Hope arises, wild and free.

Riding waves of pure zeal,
We surrender to the thrill.
Every heartbeat, so real,
Time stands still, yet we fill.

A Symphony of Sensation

Listen close to the song,
Each note a breath of life.
In this world we belong,
Harmony cuts like a knife.

Touch the fabric of dreams,
Woven with colors bright.
Every whisper redeems,
In the stillness of night.

Taste the sweetness of time,
Savored with every glance.
In the rhythm, we climb,
Lost in a timeless dance.

A symphony flows deep,
Igniting our very core.
In the echoes, we leap,
Forever longing for more.

Unfolding the Desire

In the quiet of night,
Whispers flutter like leaves.
Yearning hearts take flight,
Unraveling what deceives.

With each spark, we ignite,
Fireflies dance in the dusk.
Dreams take on new heights,
In the thrill of the musk.

Craving more than the glance,
As the stars reflect hope.
In this delicate chance,
We learn how to cope.

Unfolding the desire,
With each moment we gain.
Like a blossoming fire,
We rise above the mundane.

Glimmers of Intent

Underneath the soft glow,
Glimmers dance on the ground.
Fleeting moments we sow,
In the silence, they're found.

Like the dawn's first embrace,
Promise lingers in air.
In this sacred space,
Intentions rise, laid bare.

Each flicker a beacon bright,
Guiding paths yet to tread.
In the quiet of night,
Our hopes become the thread.

Glimmers of light, we chase,
Stitching dreams into life.
In the heart's gentle pace,
We conquer present strife.

Echoes of Enthusiasm

In whispers bright, the dreams ignite,
A spark that dances through the night.
With every cheer, the hearts align,
In hope's embrace, we intertwine.

The laughter rings, a melody,
Each moment shared, a symphony.
With courage bold, we chase the sun,
Together strong, we have begun.

In trials faced, we rise anew,
With every step, our spirits grew.
The echoes call, a vibrant song,
In unity, we all belong.

Through stormy skies, our passions soar,
With fervent hearts, we seek for more.
A journey made, with eyes that gleam,
In echoes bright, we chase the dream.

Labyrinth of Love

In corridors of tender grace,
Two souls wander in sweet embrace.
Each turn reveals a heart's delight,
In shadows cast by soft moonlight.

Oblivious to time's cruel hand,
They dance along, a secret plan.
With every glance, the whispers tease,
In tangled paths, they find their ease.

Yet doubts may creep and shadows loom,
In every heart, there's room for bloom.
Through trials faced and laughter shared,
In love's domain, they're never scared.

And at the core, a treasure lies,
In every truth, their passion flies.
With courage bold, they forge ahead,
In labyrinths, true love is fed.

Veins of Ambition

In every pulse, a goal does beat,
With every step, the path's complete.
Through trials vast, the fire grows,
In veins of strength, the fervor flows.

The mountains rise, they beckon high,
With dreams adorned, we reach the sky.
Each setback met with fierce resolve,
Within our hearts, ambitions evolve.

Through sleepless nights and endless dawns,
The brave arise, the weak withdraw.
With vision clear, we chart our fate,
In every heartbeat, we create.

In the quiet moments, we reflect,
On journeys taken, dreams collect.
With passion's fire, we find our way,
In veins of strength, we seize the day.

The Road of Recklessness

With wild abandon, we take flight,
The road ahead, a thrilling sight.
No maps to guide, just daring thrills,
In reckless joy, the spirit spills.

Beneath the stars, our laughter rings,
Chasing after the joy that clings.
Each curve we take, a leap of faith,
In freedom's arms, we find our place.

Through winding paths and distant sighs,
We dance with fate, we touch the skies.
The pulse of life, it beats so strong,
In recklessness, we find our song.

But in the shadows, caution waits,
To whisper softly of the fates.
Yet still we roam, with hearts ablaze,
On the road of life, forever we graze.

The Vibrant Quest

In dawn's embrace, we seek the light,
With every step, our dreams take flight.
Colors swirl in the morning's kiss,
A path of wonder, too sweet to miss.

Through fields of gold, and skies of blue,
Each heartbeat whispers, 'Push on through.'
With laughter as our guiding star,
We chase the magic, near and far.

Mountains rise, with voices bold,
Stories of courage waiting to be told.
In shadows thick, we'll find our way,
For every night gives birth to day.

Eager hearts in unity stand,
Together we weave, a hopeful strand.
In every quest, a treasure gained,
In vibrant hues, our souls unchained.

Shadows of Intense Awakening

In the silence, echoes scream,
Reflections dance in a waking dream.
Shadows stretch, revealing grace,
A journey hidden, each sacred space.

With every heartbeat, truth unfolds,
In whispered tones, the past retold.
A flicker bright in the dusky hue,
Awakens depths we never knew.

Lofty wishes riding the breeze,
In quiet corners, our spirits tease.
The night conceals but never denies,
The dawn will bring new, daring skies.

From darkness springs the urge to rise,
Emerging fierce with open eyes.
In shadows deep, our strength is sought,
Each fierce moment, a lesson taught.

The Color of Reckless Joy

With laughter ringing soft and clear,
We paint the world, erasing fear.
Each brushstroke wild, a splash so bright,
A tapestry woven from pure delight.

The skies explode in vibrant hues,
In reckless joy, we ignite the muse.
With spirited dance and open hearts,
We create a symphony, each note imparts.

Through fields of dreams, we spin and twirl,
Radiating warmth, our colors unfurl.
Let's chase the sunset, hand in hand,
In the rhythm of life, we boldly stand.

As stars emerge, we'll keep the song,
In every heartbeat, we belong.
With every color, our joy shines through,
Together forever, just me and you.

Designing the Unseen Map

In the quiet breath of a timeless night,
We sketch pathways, hidden from sight.
With ink of dreams on parchment fair,
We chart the course, for souls that dare.

Lines that twist and turn anew,
Revealing places for us to pursue.
With whispers of hope, we trace the lines,
In every corner, the spirit shines.

Through valleys deep and mountains high,
The unseen map unfolds, we fly.
With every mark, a journey starts,
Embracing the world, with open hearts.

A compass reads the love we feel,
In every challenge, we learn to heal.
Together we wander, hand in hand,
Designing the map of our promised land.

Milton Keynes UK
Ingram Content Group UK Ltd.
UKHW020708221024
449848UK00023B/36

9 789916 880326